101 Christmas Crafts

★ The Pat Richards Crafts Collection ★

101 Christmas Crafts

Ornaments, Decorations, and Gifts

Photography by Bill Milne

FRIEDMAN/FAIRFAX
PUBLISHERS

A FRIEDMAN/FAIRFAX BOOK

© 1996 by Michael Friedman Publishing Group, Inc.

Library of Congress Cataloging-in-Publication data available upon request.

ISBN 1-56799-340-0

Editor: Francine Hornberger
Art Director: Lynne Yeamans
Designer: Joseph Rutt
Photography Director: Christopher C. Bain
Photography by Bill Milne/New York

Color separations by Bright Arts Graphics (S) Pte Ltd
Printed and bound in Great Britain by
Butler & Tanner Ltd, Frome and London

Every effort has been made to present the information in this book in a clear, complete, and accurate manner. It is important that all instructions be clearly understood
before beginning a project. Please follow instructions carefully. Due to the variability
of materials and skills, end results may vary. The publisher and the author expressly
disclaim any and all liability resulting from injuries, damages, or other losses incurred
as a result of material presented herein. The author also suggests refraining from
using glass, beads, or buttons on crafts intended for small children.

For bulk purchases and special sales, please contact:
Friedman/Fairfax Publishers
Attention: Sales Department
15 West 26th Street
New York, New York 10010
212/685-6610   FAX 212/685-1307

Visit the Friedman/Fairfax Website:
http://www.webcom.com/friedman

This book is dedicated to every one who endured its birth

with me, especially Mark, Keith, and Lee.

A special thanks to Amy Syrell, Kenvyn Richards, and Jackie Smyth

for their help in preparing the projects.

INTRODUCTION

❖ ❖ ❖ ❖ ❖

Christmas is, personally, my favorite holiday. I spend many happy hours deliberating what I can make for whom, pondering purchases, plotting and planning months before the season arrives. With a large family and a busy lifestyle, if I don't work ahead, I'm doomed. But that's only part of the reason. I love making things, and making things for those I love is even more fun.

Before You Begin

It occurs to me that as much as I knew about crafting before I began this book project, I know a lot more now that it's done. Some of the lessons I've learned, both now and in the past, I'd like to share with you in hopes of easing your path.

Fusible adhesive—used in many of the projects—is available in several weights and each has its pluses and minuses. For the most part I've used Heat'nBond on the projects calling for fusible web in this book. The lightweight type works well for projects requiring sewing, and the regular or ultra hold is great for no-sew projects. Always test the adhesive on the fabrics you plan to use it on. If you find your machine gumming up when sewing though the adhesive, regular applications of Sewer's Aid, a lubricant that can be applied to needle and thread, eases the process tremendously.

When working with metallic threads, the use of sewing machine needles specially made for metallic threads cuts down on fraying and breaking.

Occasionally you may be tempted to glue on a trim instead of sewing it, a frequently tedious procedure. I urge you to test the method before committing yourself. If the project is destined for repeated use, as well as being laundered or folded for storage, glue may not hold up.

I would like to thank several corporations for providing materials for use in this book. The Beadery was very generous in providing beads for the key chains and eyeglass chain projects as well as for the Victorian garland.

The Kittrich Corporation provided the Iron-on Clear Cote for the fabric lunch bag and kids' art frame projects.

The Wm. E. Wright Company was kind enough to provide a wide range of their cords, ribbons and tassels, which ended up on all sorts of projects including the ribbon pouch ornaments, the heart shaped bookmark, the flower bouquet ornaments and the guest towels.

Duncan has supplied me with a selection of products, and most of the painted items in this book have been painted with Duncan Decorator Acrylics.

Part One

AN ELEGANT

CHRISTMAS

ORNAMENTS

Crown Ornament

❖ ❖ ❖ ❖ ❖

Glittering with jewels and bright gold metallic foiled cardboard over rich dark burgundy velveteen, these tiny crowns will add a touch of royal majesty to your holiday.

Materials:

Gold metallic cardboard

24 gauge craft wire

7-inch (18cm) square of burgundy velveteen

Assorted rhinestones, pearls, and gold beads

Matching thread

Gold paint (optional)

Compass

Glue

Trace and cut out pattern pieces for crown band and lining band. Using a ruler, draft a cross with arms of equal length, each ⅜ inch (1cm) wide and 2¾ inches (7cm) long. Using a straight pin or needle, trace each of these pattern pieces onto the gold cardboard and cut out, following traced lines. If desired, paint the cut edges of the crown band with gold paint. Overlap the edges of crown band and glue in place.

Cut two pieces of wire each 11¼ inches (28.5cm) long. Fold each in half and twist the two folded pieces together once at the midpoint of each, making a cross. Glue the wire to the wrong side of cardboard cross. When dry, gently shape cross to form top of crown and glue ends to the inside of crown band about ¼ inch (6mm) above lower edge, centering each end behind one of the large decorative points on the crown band.

With a compass, draft a circle 6¼ inches (16cm) in diameter. Using circle

pattern, cut one from velveteen. Work a running stitch just inside the edge of velveteen circle, draw up stitches to circumference of crown and fasten off. Fit velveteen inside crown and glue edges to inside of crown band, having edge of velveteen about ¼ inch (6mm) above lower edge.

Curl lining band slightly to ease fit inside crown. This band will be glued to the inside of crown band to cover the raw edges of velveteen the longer (outside curved) edge will be the edge to match to the bottom edge of crown band. Glue lining band to inside crown band, wrong sides together.

Decorate crown with pearls and/or rhinestones glued in place as desired. Top crown with a few gold beads (I used an 8mm gold ring, topped with an 11 × 9mm gold pyramid bead and a small gold round bead). Cut an 8-inch (20.5cm) length of gold cord, thread through crown and knot ends for hanger.

1 square = 1 inch   Enlarge 114%

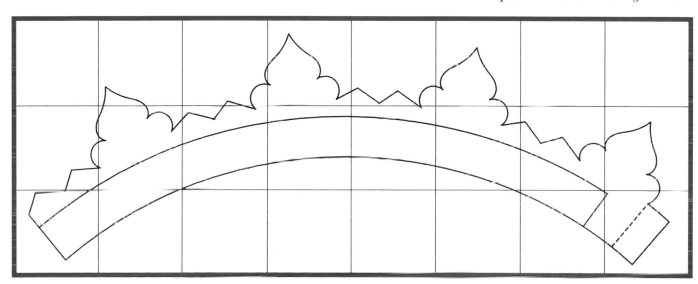

Embroidered Heart Ornament

❖ ❖ ❖ ❖ ❖

*Crazy quilting, a great favorite with Victorian women for showing off embroidery skills, is used here
to create tiny heart-shaped keepsakes to hang on your tree or
to decorate a gift box.*

Materials:

**Scraps of men's ties (thrift shops are
a good source for old ties)**

**Gold metallic machine
embroidery thread**

Fiberfill stuffing

Gold metallic cord

**Assorted beads, tassels and
other trims**

Beading needle (optional)

**Sewing machine with
decorative stitch**

With right sides together and using a narrow seam, stitch together several pieces of tie fabrics. Press seams open. Set machine to a decorative stitch and using metallic thread, stitch over seams having the gold thread on right side of fabric.

Trace and cut out heart pattern adding ¼ inch (6mm) seam allowance. Place pattern on assembled fabric with a decorative seam running through it at some point and cut out. Cut a second heart for back from same fabric or undecorated fabric. With right sides together, sew a ¼-inch (6mm) seam around all sides leaving an opening for turning. Clip curves and turn right side out. Stuff, then slipstitch opening closed.

Trim as desired, using patterns on fabric for inspiration, or working from your own imagination. Cut an 8-inch (20.5cm) piece of gold cord. Knot ends together. Stitch center of loop to top notch of heart ornament for hanging loop.

To work a beaded motif: anchor thread and pick up two or three beads on needle. Insert needle into ornament and bring it up between last and next to last bead just worked. Bring needle through last bead and pick up two more. Continue to add beads to design going back through last bead worked each time before adding new ones. Anchor thread at end of work and bring needle up a short distance away before cutting thread.

To work the scalloped beaded border: anchor thread at edge of ornament. Pick up five seed beads with needle and anchor them to ornament edge by taking a couple of tiny stitches about ¼ inch (6mm) farther along. Continue picking up beads and anchoring them to the edge every ¼ inch (6mm), all the way around the ornament.

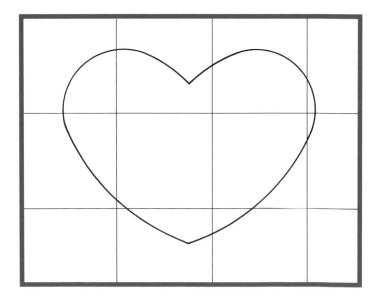

1 square = 1 inch   Pattern at 100%

Victorian Garland

❖ ❖ ❖ ❖ ❖

A multitude of bright and shiny gold beads alternating with silk-scrap-covered foam beads, trimmed with gold braid makes for a sumptuous garland with which to wrap your Victorian-style tree.

Materials:

For approximately 3 feet (91.5cm) of garland you will need:

8 Styrofoam® balls each 1 inch (2.5cm) in diameter

Assorted scraps of men's ties

Assorted gold metallic trims

Gold metallic beads: 32 pony beads

16 19 × 6 mm spaghetti beads

16 14mm melon beads

16 8mm round beads

8 18mm sunburst beads

1 large bead for either end of garland

Heavy-duty thread (carpet or upholstery thread, dental floss, etc.)

Large-eyed needle

Pliers

Serrated knife

Glue

Cut tie scraps into circles approximately 2 inches (5cm) in diameter; you will need two for each ball. With a serrated knife, cut each ball in half. Spread glue on flat side of cut ball and center unglued side on wrong side of fabric circle. Pull edges of fabric tightly around the half ball and push into the glue and into the Styrofoam as well, depressing the inside center of ball. This will make room for the excess fabric at the center of the ball. Repeat with other half of the ball, then glue the two halves back together, pressing tightly. Hold the two halves together with a rubber band until the glue has dried. Apply a strip of glue to the seam between the two halves and wrap with gold trim.

Cut a piece of heavy-duty thread approximately 2 yards (1.8m) long and thread into a large-eyed needle. Thread a large bead onto doubled thread length, and tie ends to main body of thread to form an anchor for the garland. Trim ends and glue to the thread. Slide on beads in the following order: pony bead, spaghetti bead, pony bead, melon bead, round bead, sunburst, round bead, melon bead, pony bead, spaghetti bead, pony bead, and then one of the covered balls. Pliers may help in pulling the needle through. Repeat this pattern until your garland reaches the desired length.

When it becomes necessary to add a new length of thread, a good place to do it is right after the first spaghetti bead. Tie the new length on about ¼-inch (6mm) from the last bead, trim the ends to ¼-inch (6mm) and glue them to the thread. The knot and ends will be concealed inside the next beads added. At the end of the garland wrap and tie thread around the remaining large bead, and knot, trim and glue the ends, concealing them inside previous beads.

Rose Bouquet Ornament

❖ ❖ ❖ ❖ ❖

Traditionally a symbol of love and passion, these small bouquets of roses, created from either satin or velvet ribbon, will add a warm and vivid touch of red to your Christmas tree.

Materials:

Satin bouquet: 1½ yards (1.37m) of 1½-inch (4cm) wide and 1 yard (91.5cm) of ⅞-inch (2cm) wide red satin ribbon, ¼ yard (23cm) of 1½-inch (4cm) wide green satin ribbon, 24-gauge wire

Velvet bouquet: 1 yard (30.5cm) of 1½-inch (4cm) wide and ¾ yard (68.5cm) of ⅞-inch (2cm) wide dark red velvet ribbon, ⅓ yard (30.5cm) of 1½-inch (4cm) wide green satin ribbon

Matching thread

Either bouquet: 28 gauge wire, floral tape, gold bouquet holder (available from D. Blümchen) or make your own from a gold doily, scrap of green felt

Glue

Satin bouquet For each flower: from wider red ribbon cut one 4½-inch (11.5cm) piece and four pieces each 4¼-inches (11cm) long; from narrow red ribbon cut four pieces each 2½ inches (6.5cm). For each bud: From wider red ribbon, cut one 4½-inch (11.5cm) piece and from narrow red ribbon cut four pieces each 2½-inch (11.5cm) Fold and wrap the 4½-inch (11.5cm) piece into a tight bud and secure base by wrapping with 28 gauge wire. Do not cut wire, you will attach petals with same wire.

Take each 2½-inch (6.5cm) piece and fold in half, wrong sides together. Tuck upper corners into petal and glue in place. Glue edges together. Do the same with each 4¼-inch (11cm) piece. Cut a 5½-inch (14cm) piece of wire, bend into petal shape and insert inside each large petal. Beginning with the smaller petals and pleating bottom as necessary, place two petals at a time around bud and wrap with wire to secure. When all petals have been secured, cut wire, leaving a long tail. Fold and twist tail to make a stem about 4 inches (10cm) long. Make two large roses as described above, then one small rose, following the same directions, attaching small petals only, then create a stem with tail end of wire. Hold roses and bud together and twist stems together.

Cut two pieces of green ribbon each 3 inches (7.5cm) long. With wrong side facing up, fold one end back ½ inch

(1.5cm). Fold each corner into center and overlap slightly to form pointed tip of leaf. Glue overlapped corners together. Pinch opposite end together to form leaf and secure with 28 gauge wire, leaving a tail for stem same as for flowers. Repeat for second leaf. Position leaves on bouquet as desired and wrap leaf stems around bouquet stem.

Slip stem through hole in bouquet holder and glue holder against base of flowers and leaves. When glue is dry, fold up ends of stem, leaving about 3 inches (7.5cm) with which to secure bouquet to tree. Wrap stem with floral tape. Cut a half circle, approximately 2 inches (5cm) across, of green felt. Wrap, trimming as necessary, and glue in place around base of bouquet holder.

Velvet bouquet For central bud, cut a 2-inch (5cm) piece of 1½-inch (4cm) wide ribbon, cut petals the same sizes as for satin flowers, with large roses having two small and four large petals.

Bud is created the same way as for satin roses, but petals are folded in half with right sides together and sewn along sides and top to create petal shape, then turned right side out. Complete flowers in same manner as for satin roses except that velvet bouquet is made up of one large rose and two small ones.

Make three leaves same as for satin bouquet and complete velvet bouquet in same manner as for satin bouquet.

Crazy Quilt Ball

❖ ❖ ❖ ❖ ❖

Deceptively elegant, this ornament is extremely easy to create.
Scraps of colorful silks and gold braids transform ordinary Styrofoam balls
into extravagant decorations.

Materials:

3-inch (7.5cm) Styrofoam ball

Assorted scraps of silk (old ties are a good source)

Assorted scraps of gold trims

½ yard (45.5cm) of ⅛-inch (3mm) wide gold braid

White glue

Small screwdriver

Place a small, approximately 2 to 4-inch (5 to 10cm) square of silk over a portion of the ball. Using the screwdriver and beginning ⅛ (3mm) to ¼ (6mm) inch from edge of scrap, poke edges of fabric into ball. Align a second scrap of fabric with one edge of first piece and poke abutting edge into the same ditch; continue around second piece until all edges are tucked into foam. Continue with additional scraps of fabric, trimming pieces as necessary until ball is completely covered with fabric. Glue pieces of gold trim over adjoining seams, changing styles of trim as desired from seam to seam.

Fold an 18-inch (45.5cm) length of gold braid in half and knot 3½ inches (9cm) from fold. Tie a double (total of four loops) bow at knot and glue bow to top of ball, putting additional glue on knot to secure. If necessary, hold knot in place with a straight pin until glue is dry.

DECORATIONS

Display Plate

❖ ❖ ❖ ❖ ❖

*Christmas cakes and cookies will look even more tempting when displayed on your
"one-of-a-kind" holiday plate, the creation of which is a terrific way to make use of all
those beautiful holiday cards and papers you couldn't bear to throw away.*

Materials:

Clear glass plate

**Paper designs, scrap art, gift wrap,
metallic doilies**

Decoupage medium or white glue

**Polyurethane or other water-
proof finish**

0000 steel wool

Acrylic paint in desired colors

Paintbrush

Trim paper designs, scrap art, gift wrap, and metallic doilies and arrange on plate. Transfer pieces to another surface and clean and dry back of glass plate. Working from foreground to background, apply an even coat of decoupage medium or white glue to front of art and smooth in place on back of plate. When all pieces have dried, apply a light coat of decoupage medium or glue to pieces and let dry. Sand edges of paper art lightly with steel wool and apply a second coat of medium or glue. When plate is dry, apply at least two coats of acrylic paint, letting each dry before applying the next. Sand edges with steel wool. Finish the plate with two or more coats of polyurethane, letting each coat dry completely and sanding lightly with steel wool between coats.

Butterfly Sachet

❖ ❖ ❖ ❖ ❖

*Luxurious trinkets, like this sachet shaped like a delicate butterfly and filled
with fragrant reminders of spring, were favored items for the Victorians to create
and to give—a gift which today would be equally appreciated.*

Materials:

**Two pieces each approximately 9 ×
8 inches (23 × 20.5cm) of ivory satin**

**8 × 6-inch (20.5 × 15cm) piece of
ivory lace**

**Two 8 × 6-inch (20.5 × 15cm) pieces
of tear away stabilizer**

**Gold metallic machine
embroidery thread**

Gold metallic paint

Potpourri, mostly petals

Ivory tassel

Air erasable marker

Small sharp scissors

Sewing machine with zigzag stitch

Trace and cut out pattern. Transfer markings to ivory satin with air erasable marker. With gold thread in needle and white in bobbin, set machine for medium width zigzag and loosen top tension slightly. With a piece of stabilizer supporting work, satin stitch along the outline of butterfly wings and body. Remove the stabilizer. Make a sandwich of butterfly right side up on top of the lace, on top of the second piece of stabilizer. Pin pieces together to prevent shifting. With white thread in both needle and bobbin and machine set on a slightly narrower zigzag, satin stitch around shapes inside each wing. Remove

stabilizer. Using small, sharp scissors, very carefully cut the satin away from the inside of the shapes just outlined. With gold paint, fill in butterfly body and head. Allow to dry.

Right sides together, lay completed sachet front on top of remaining piece of satin and pin around the edges. Stitch ¼ inch (6mm) outside outlining satin stitch, leaving an opening for turning and stuffing. Trim seam allowance to ¼ inch (6mm), clip curves and corners. Turn and press. Stuff sachet with potpourri petals and slip stitch opening closed. Wrap top of tassel with gold thread, gluing ends to secure. Tack tassel to bottom of butterfly body.

1 square = 1 inch   Pattern at 100%

Crazy Quilt Eyeglass Case

❖ ❖ ❖ ❖ ❖

Employing machine embroidery and gold metallic thread to imitate the look of authentic crazy quilting greatly simplifies the construction of this eyeglass case, giving it an ornate look without the time-consuming hand work.

Materials:

15 × 8½-inch (38 × 21.5cm) piece of muslin

Scraps from old ties

Gold metallic thread for machine sewing

15 × 8½-inch (38 × 21.5cm) piece of fusible fleece

15 × 8½-inch (38 × 21.5cm) piece of black cotton knit fabric

Small black Velcro dot

Sewing machine with decorative stitch

Avoiding perfectly square and rectangular shapes, select first tie scrap, pin to center of muslin base and baste around all edges. Place next scrap, right sides together, on top of first piece matching one edge. Pin and baste along that edge. Press scrap back over seam, pin remaining edges to muslin base and baste in place. Continue overlapping scraps and basting in place to muslin base until entire piece is covered. When you are working into a corner, baste the longer edge right sides together, then turn under the raw edge on second side and baste in place over raw edge of previously applied patch.

With gold thread in needle, and machine set for a decorative stitch, stitch over seams on right side of patchwork, using different stitches for adjoining seams. Combinations of stitches can expand the limited selection found on many machines.

Following manufacturer's directions, fuse fleece to wrong side of black knit fabric. Enlarge pattern for eyeglass case (page 54) and add ¼-inch (6mm) seam allowance all around. Cut one from fleece/knit piece and one from assembled crazy quilt piece. With right sides of pieces together, sew around all edges with a ¼-inch (6mm) seam, leaving about 3 inches (7.5cm) open on one side for turning. Clip corners and into inside corners. Turn right side out and press. Fold in raw edges and slipstitch opening closed. Fold lower edge up at point indicated on pattern and slip stitch edges together, leaving about ½ inch (1.5cm) open at fold on one side.

Insert end of gold cord into opening at fold and slipstitch cord to seam line around the sides and top edges of case, then along the fold line at lower edge of case back to starting point. Cut cord and slip end into opening, securing cord and closing the opening around cord ends. Attach hook portion of Velcro dot to bottom front of case and loop portion to the inside of top flap.

Part Two

A HOMESPUN

CHRISTMAS

ORNAMENTS

Paper Bag Ornament

❖ ❖ ❖ ❖ ❖

*A miniature and very charming version of the utilitarian brown paper
shopping bag, these charming little sacks will hang on your tree ready to be filled
with candies or tiny gifts.*

Materials:

**Brown kraft paper, 4 × 8½ inches
(10 × 21.5cm) for each ornament**

Scraps of red paper

Assorted buttons, 2 per ornament

Red embroidery floss

Jute twine

Glue

Fold up 1 inch (2.5cm) along long edge of kraft paper for bottom of bag. Along top edge, mark off five vertical sections: 2, 1½, 2½, 1½, and 2 inches (5, 4, 6.5, 4 and 5cm). Beginning at one end, fold up at first mark, making sure to align top edges and creasing only as far as to the bottom fold. Make a second fold in the same manner at the next mark. Now bring these two folds together, pinching the area in between accordion-style. As you crease the fold toward the bottom, a triangular fold will begin to form which will force the bottom of the bag up as on grocery store bags. If you are having trouble, open the folds and mark lines at a 45-degree angle from the side folds to the center fold and try again.

Work this same folding procedure at the opposite end of the bag. Lap the edges along center back and glue. Fold bottom up and glue in place.

Cut a 2¾-inch (7cm) square of red paper. Cut a freehand heart from the square. Glue the heart to the front of one bag, the square it was cut from to another. Cut a 9-inch (23cm) length of twine and knot each end. With embroidery floss, sew one button to one side of bag front, sewing over one end of twine on the inside. Tie off floss and reinforce knot with glue. Repeat with other button on opposite side of bag front. Cut a 10-inch (25.5cm) length of twine. Poke a hole on either side of bag back at approximately the same location where handle is attached to front. Thread jute through holes and knot ends. Reinforce knots with glue.

Snowman Ornament

❖ ❖ ❖ ❖ ❖

*Odds and ends of embroidery floss, paint, a pinch of clay and two twigs
transform leftover scraps of plain cotton batting into everyone's favorite symbol of
an abundant winter snowfall.*

Size:
4 inches (10cm) tall

Materials:
Scraps of natural cotton batting

Fiberfill stuffing

**Off-white embroidery floss, J. & P.
Coats #5933**

**Orange oven-hardening polymer
clay or orange fabric paint**

**Black fabric paint in a squeeze
bottle applicator**

Twigs

**Small piece of ribbon or twill tape
for hanger**

From orange clay, form a small carrot nose, approximately ½-inch (1.5cm) long. Bake according to manufacturer's directions.

Use pattern to cut two snowmen from cotton batting. With six strands of embroidery floss, work blanket stitch around outside edges through both pieces, stuffing lightly before closing seam.

With black fabric paint apply eyes and buttons. When paint has dried, glue nose in place or paint nose in with fabric paint. Cut twigs approximately 1¼ inches (3cm) long for arms. Use the point of a scissor to poke a hole in the top layer of batting, insert twig arm and glue in place. Glue or sew a small loop of ribbon or twill tape to back of snowman's head for hanging.

If desired, add a scarf, top hat or other trims cut from felt or fabric scraps.

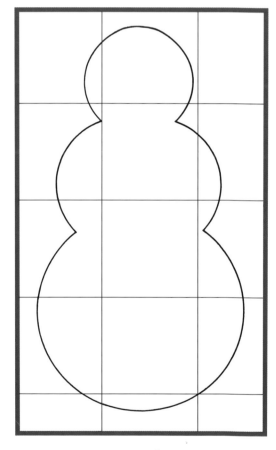

1 square = 1 inch Pattern at 100%

DECORATIONS

Natural Garland

(Environmentally Friendly Craft)

❖ ❖ ❖ ❖ ❖

*Nature supplies a variety of interesting seed pods or nuts. By drilling a hole through
and stringing them alternately with gold beads you can make a simple but striking
garland to accent your tree or other holiday decorations.*

Materials:

**Dried seedpods (I used prickly ball-
shaped pods from the sweet gum
tree)**

**Wooden beads, ½-inch (1.5cm)
diameter**

Metallic gold paint

**Heavyduty thread or string for
stringing garland**

Large-eyed needle

Glue

**Drill (unless you find some sort
of pod that you can pierce with
a needle or nail, your seedpods will
need to be drilled for stringing)**

Paint wooden beads with gold metallic paint and allow to dry. I find it helpful to thread the beads onto a chenille stem to facilitate painting. Drill a hole in each seedpod large enough for threaded needle to pass through. To preserve the points of the pods, we hammered three nails through a thin scrap of wood to form a tripod on which the pod could rest, then we drilled a hole through the center of the pod. It is very helpful to then string the pod immediately, with at least an interim piece of string, so you do not have to spend time looking for the hole when you are ready to assemble the garland.

With a doubled length of string threaded through needle, thread on the first gold bead and tie a knot securely around it to anchor the garland. Apply a dot of glue to secure the knot. Thread one pod and one bead alternately until garland measures desired length. Add additional lengths of string by knotting them at a point which will be hidden inside a pod or bead and applying glue to the knot before trimming ends. When finished stringing garland, knot again around the last bead, glue knot and trim ends.

Wooden Sleigh Candle Holder

❖ ❖ ❖ ❖ ❖

*This simply shaped wooden sleigh is painted a bright red with a country-crackle finish
or, if you desire, accent the edges with gold, for a brighter touch when tucked in
among sprigs of holiday greenery.*

Materials:

**⅜-inch (1cm) pine stock,
approximately 6 × 7 inches (15 ×
18cm) (basswood or poplar may
be substituted)**

**Scrap of ¾-inch (2cm) pine stock
(or one of the substitutes
mentioned above)**

4 1-inch (2.5cm) #17 wire brads

**Medium brown and country red
acrylic paint**

Crackle finish

Matte sealer

100 grit sandpaper

Tools Required:

**Machine jigsaw or hand coping saw
for sides of sleigh**

**Machine jigsaw or hand crosscut
saw for base of sleigh**

**Electric drill with ¾-inch (2cm)
spade bit or bit brace and
¾-inch (2cm) auger bit**

Trace pattern and transfer twice to ⅜-inch (1cm) stock. Using jigsaw or coping saw, cut out pieces. Sand edges.

Using jigsaw or crosscut saw cut a 1¾-inch (4.5cm) square from ¾-inch (2cm) stock. Mark center of square piece. Drill hole for candle ¾ inch (2cm) in diameter to a depth of ⅝ inch (1.5cm). Position square, candle hole up, between bases of sleigh sides taking care that it does not show above runners, and glue in place. Reinforce glue with nails through sides of sleigh into candle holder square approximately ⅜-inch (1cm) from edges of square. Fill nail holes, if desired, and sand any remaining rough edges.

Paint candle holder with brown paint. When dry, apply a smooth, even coat of crackle finish and let dry according to manufacturer's directions before applying red paint. When thoroughly dry, apply two coats of matte sealer allowing first coat to dry completely before applying the second.

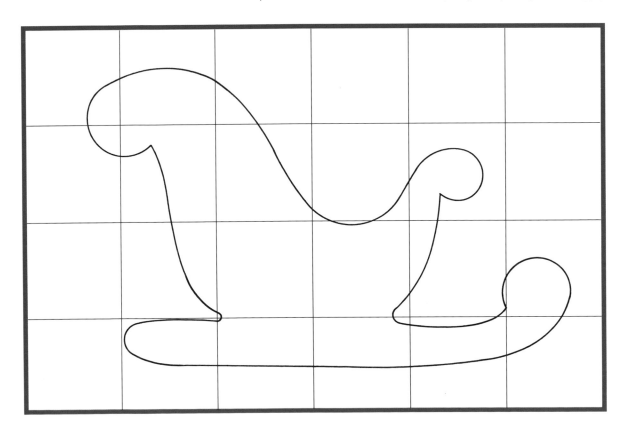

1 square = 1 inch   Pattern at 100%

Magnetic Checkers

❖ ❖ ❖ ❖ ❖

*Paint and buttons in bright Christmas colors transform a magnetic board designed
for holding needlework charts into a jaunty checkerboard, especially well-suited
for games on the go.*

Materials:

**Magnetic board (sold in craft stores
for holding needlework directions)**

Red and green acrylic paint

Masking tape, ¾ inch (2cm) wide

Sponge paint applicator

Fine point brush

Clear finish

**16 each red and green buttons,
assorted**

32 small round magnets

Glue

With a pencil, lightly mark a 6-inch (15cm) square in the center of magnetic board. Divide the square into ¾-inch (2cm) squares. Cut masking tape into ¾-inch (2cm) squares and cover every other square on the board. Also mask outside of square. With sponge applicator, sponge uncovered squares red. Set aside to dry. Remove the masking tape and carefully repeat the process with green paint on the remaining squares. Transfer tree pattern to lightweight cardboard and cut out. Trace tree three times, evenly spaced, across each edge of board. With fine point brush, paint trees alternately red and green. Remove any remaining pencil lines and if desired, coat entire board with clear finish. Glue magnets to backs of buttons.

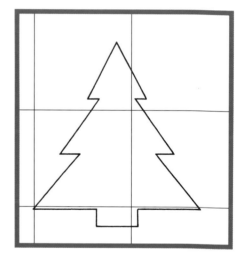

1 square =1 inch   Pattern at 100%

Child's Striped Hat and Mittens

❖ ❖ ❖ ❖ ❖

This very easy-to-knit hat looks particularly charming on children, and when paired with coordinating mittens in warm wool, the set makes a gift all mothers will appreciate, even if the kids don't.

Size:

Hat is one size fits all; Mittens are medium, changes for small are in parentheses.

Materials:

2 100 gram (3½ oz) balls Knitaly by Lane Borgosesia in charcoal, 1 ball in red

Knitting needles size 3 and 5 (3.25mm/10 and 4mm/8)

Crochet hook size F (4mm/8)

Stitch holder or safety pin

Stitch markers

Gauge:

5 sts = 1 inch (2.5cm)

Abbreviations:

k=knit, p=purl, st st=stockinette stitch, st=stitch, tog=together, sl=slip, inc=increase

Hat

With larger needles and charcoal, cast on 82 sts. Work in st st (K right side rows, P wrong side rows) for 14 rows. *Change to red and work 4 rows. Change to charcoal and work 8 rows. Repeat from * once. ** Change to red and work 4 rows, then work 10 rows in charcoal. Repeat from ** once. Change to red and work 4 rows, then work 12 rows in charcoal, 4 rows in red, then 8 rows of charcoal. Slip 41 sts to another needle. Hold work, folded in half, right sides together. K 2 tog (1 st from each needle) all the way across, binding off as you go. Sew side seam of hat, reversing seam along bottom 2 to 3 inches (5 to 7.6cm) so edge can roll naturally to right side.

For one tassel, cut approximately thirty-three lengths of red yarn each 8 inches (20.5cm) long. Fold strands in half to find the middle and tie another strand around tightly at that point. Beginning about ½-inch (1.5cm) from fold, with another strand of red yarn, wrap several times around tassel, securing end under the wrapping. When wrapped area measures about ¼-inch (6mm), cut yarn leaving a tail and pull tail under wraps and up through tassel. Trim ends. Make another tassel in the same manner. Attach red yarn to top of one tassel and with crochet hook work a chain approximately 12 inches (30.5cm) long. Attach chain to one top corner of hat. Repeat with remaining tassel and attach to opposite corner. Tie chained strings to draw corners of hat together.

Mittens

With smaller needles and red, cast on (32) 36 sts. Work in k 2, p 2 rib for 3 inches (7.6cm), decrease (1) 3 sts on last row—(31) 33 sts. Change to larger needles and charcoal. Beginning with a right side row, work in st st for 4 rows.

Next row: Shape thumb: K (14) 15 sts, sl marker onto needle, M 1 (pick up strand between sts on row below and place on left hand needle, k through back of strand), k 3, M 1, sl marker onto needle, k to end. Work 1 row even. Continue to work increases for thumb as before until there are 9 sts between markers. Change to red and continue as before until there are 13 sts between markers. Change to charcoal and work 3 more rows.

Next Row: Work to thumb sts, sl these 13 sts onto holder, finish row. Work even in st st until piece measures (5) 6 inches (12.7/15.2cm) above cuff; at same time, work in pattern of 4 rows red, 10 rows charcoal, end with a wrong side row.

Next row: *K 2 tog, k 2; repeat from * across. P one row.

Next row: *K 2 tog, k 1; repeat from * across. P one row.

Next row: K 2 tog across. Cut yarn leaving a long tail. Thread tail through remaining sts and fasten off.

Return thumb sts to needle. Work in color pattern as for mitten for 1½ inches (4cm) above dividing row, inc 2 sts on first row. Work last 2 decrease rows same as for mitten hand. End off. Sew thumb and hand seams, reversing seam on last 1¼ inches (3cm) of cuff so it can be folded back.

Snowman Pin

❖ ❖ ❖ ❖ ❖

A petite 2½ inches (6.5cm) tall, this little guy has to be one of the smallest snowmen around! And thanks to the pin on his back you can wear him on your lapel to show everyone that you're feeling the holiday spirit.

Size:
2½ inches (6.5cm) tall

Materials:
3 inch (7.5cm) square of natural cotton batting or natural color felt

Off-white embroidery floss

Small amount fiberfill stuffing

Scraps of black felt

Black and orange fabric paint

Small twigs

Pin back

1 square = 1 inch   Pattern at 100%

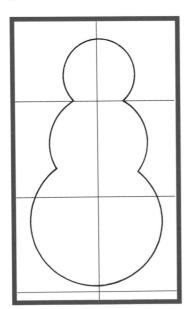

Trace and cut out pattern for snowman. Cut two snowmen from batting. With embroidery floss, and holding both snowman pieces together, work blanket stitch around all edges, stopping before finishing to stuff lightly. With black fabric paint, apply eyes, mouth and buttons. With orange paint, make a triangular-shaped carrot nose between eyes and mouth.

From black felt cut an oval hat brim approximately ¾ × 1 inch (2 × 2.5cm) and a ½ × 1⅞-inch (1.5 × 5cm) strip for crown. Overlap ends of strip by ¼ inch (6mm) and glue together. Cut a small center hole in brim to fit snowman's head. Glue crown to brim and check appearance on snowman. If necessary, trim edge of brim and/or top of crown. Cut a small piece of felt to fit inside top of crown and glue in place. Glue finished hat to head of snowman. Make hole on either side of snowman body with a small sharp scissors for placement of arms. Apply glue to end of twig and insert in hole.

Affix pin back to back of completed snowman, with glue gun or sewing by hand.

Felt Button Covers

❖ ❖ ❖ ❖

These smart looking button covers are a breeze to make with purchased button cover blanks, bright shades of felt and contrasting embroidery. Together they make a fashion accent that will jazz up any shirt in your wardrobe.

Size:
Approximately 1¼ inches (3cm) in diameter

Materials:
Assorted scraps of felt

Embroidery floss, assorted colors

Purchased blank button covers

Glue (preferably one for use with jewelry)

Lightweight cardboard

Trace around a small circular object onto lightweight cardboard to draw two circles, one approximately ⅞ inch (2cm) and one approximately 1¼ inches (3cm) in diameter. Cut them out. Trace smaller circle onto felt, but don't cut out. In center of circle with six strands of embroidery floss work a small lazy daisy flower. With a second color of floss, work four French knots in the center of flower; do not cut floss. Trace larger circle onto another scrap of felt; do not cut out. Trim embroidered circle just inside marking and place in center of larger circle. Use floss from French knots to blanket stitch smaller circle to larger one. Trim around the edge of larger circle, just inside the line, and blanket stitch around edges with a third color of floss. Glue completed piece to button cover.

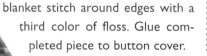

ORNAMENTS

Paper Bird

❖ ❖ ❖ ❖ ❖

*Bring a bit of the wild outdoors to your Christmas tree with these simple graphic
bird ornaments you can make with some colored paper and a little assistance
from your local copy shop.*

Materials:

Heavy paper

White craft glue

Colored pencils, paints, or markers

Nylon monofilament thread

Note: Access to a copy machine is required.

Take book to a copy shop and enlarge and copy pattern to the appropriate colored paper (or white if necessary). Color bird with markers, pencils, or paint, following color photograph. Beaks should be black or dark gray, and for cardinal, the area behind the crest should be gray; for blue jay, the area below the eye and between the beak and the black stripe should be white, the outermost portion of the tail and the inner tier of wing feathers should be tipped with white. Cut the pieces apart carefully, saving colored paper scraps, and glue all but one body piece to heavy paper. When glue has dried, cut out close to lines of wing and tail pieces and glue reverse sides to scraps of colored copy paper (or cut on lines and color in reverse sides). Cut out remaining body pieces on lines and glue the two together matching edges and trimming if necessary. Cut slits on body, tail and wings and assemble bird, enlarging slits, if necessary, to accommodate the bulk of the assembled pieces. Make a small hole on back of bird and thread with monofilament for hanging.

Papier Mâché Heads

❖ ❖ ❖ ❖ ❖

A good project for children who really love getting their hands dirty with papier mache, these heads are made around balloons and will be charming no matter how primitive the painting.

Materials:

Small round balloons

Newspapers torn into small pieces

Plain newsprint torn into small pieces

Wallpaper paste

Acrylic paints in desired colors

Clear spray fixative

Approximately 22 1-inch (2.5cm) pom-poms for clown

Approximately 25 yards (23m) brown tapestry yarn for clown

Twill tape

Cotton balls

Nylon monofilament thread

Hot glue gun

Clown

Inflate balloon to diameter of approximately 4½ inches (11.5cm). Mix wallpaper paste to a jellylike consistency, dip newspaper scraps into paste, and smooth over entire surface of balloon, leaving only the knotted end of balloon protruding (Note: This end will form point for hat). Let first layer dry completely, cover at least once more with newspaper, then at least once with plain newsprint. Crumple and saturate with paste a larger piece of plain newsprint and shape into a ball. Affix to approximate position of nose on front of covered balloon. Cover nose with small pieces of plain newsprint, smoothing them as much as possible. When nose has dried, give head one last coat of plain newsprint and let dry.

Pop and remove balloon. Paint clown as desired, or follow the photograph. I painted green stars for eyes, with blue centers and black irises. A small dot of white highlights each eye. The mouth was painted pink with a black center line. A white squiggly line was painted down one side of the hat with a lime green dot on one side of it.

When all the paint is dry, spray the head with two coats of clear fixative. Cut a 5-inch (13cm) length of nylon monofilament, tape the ends together to make a loop and glue ends to inside of balloon top.

Cut an 11 × 1½ inch (28 × 4cm) piece of cardboard. Wind yarn around and push together to create a strip of loops that measures about 9 inches (23cm) long. Glue a piece of twill tape along one side near the top. Slide loops off and glue tape to clown head just below edge of hat. Hot glue pom-poms to hat edge hiding top of yarn loops. Glue one pom-pom to top of hat covering hole where hanger is glued.

Santa

Repeat instructions for making the clown, except make the nose smaller, up to painting. Paint Santa's face pink and hat red. Paint eyes in desired color with black irises. Paint mouth dark pink. Add nylon monofilament hanger same as for clown. Glue cotton balls around brim of hat, under nose and chin and back of head for hair. Glue cotton ball to top of hat to cover hole.

Tree Stocking

❖ ❖ ❖ ❖ ❖

Easy to make from felt and scraps of lamé, the bold representation of a tree adorned with metallic glass balls decorating this stocking will lend a most cheerful spot of color to your mantelpiece.

Size:
12 to 14 inches (30.5 to 35.5cm)

Materials:
½ yard (45.5cm) each of yellow and green felt

Scraps of red, orange, green and purple lamé

Scraps of lightweight batting

Fabric glue (must be a fabric glue that can be sewn through)

Nylon machine sewing thread

¾ × 17-inch (2 × 43cm) strip of fusible adhesive

Sewing machine with zigzag stitch

Enlarge and cut out stocking pattern, adding ¼-inch (6mm) seam allowance around side and bottom edges, and a 1-inch (2.5cm) hem allowance across top edge. Cut two stockings from yellow felt. Enlarge tree pattern and cut one from green felt, adding seam allowance on stocking edges. Aligning outside edges, lay tree shape over one stocking shape. Pin tree branch edges to stocking. With machine set for a medium-width zigzag and threaded with nylon thread as top thread, stitch tree branch edges to yellow background. Trim away excess yellow felt from behind tree, taking care not to cut into tree itself. Cut six circles each 1½ inches (4cm) in diameter from lamé. Cut six slightly smaller circles from batting. Glue one batting circle beneath each lamé circle and glue to tree. When glue has dried, zigzag around edges using nylon as top thread. With right sides together, stitch stocking front to back ¼ inch (6mm) inside side and bottom edges. Trim curves and turn right side out. Fuse strip of adhesive to wrong side of top edge. Fold top 1 inch (2.5cm) to inside and fuse hem in place. Cut a 1½ × 6 inch (4 × 15cm) strip of green felt. Fold long edges to meet in center and stitch along each edge. Fold strip in half and stitch securely to inside top edge of stocking for hanging loop.

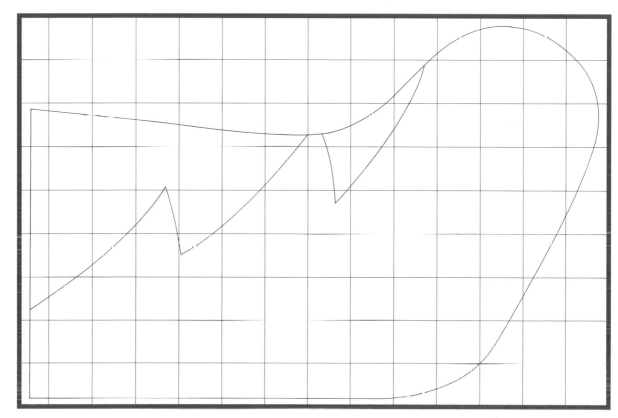

1 square = 1 inch   Enlarge to 289%

Train Candle Holder

❖ ❖ ❖ ❖ ❖

*A child's train or small model train painted with bold primary colors will become
a colorful accent for your holiday decorations when you glue several
candle cups to the tops of the cars.*

Materials:

**Small unpainted train (mine was a
kit that had to be assembled, cars
measure 3½ to 4½ inches [9 to
11.5cm] long)**

**6 candle cups to hold ½-inch
(1.5cm) candles**

Several colors of acrylic paint

Small paintbrush

Glue

Fine sandpaper (optional)

Clear sealer

If you are assembling the train, you may wish to paint the pieces before putting them together.

If the train has any kind of finish on it or if the surface is rough, sand it with a fine gauge sandpaper before proceeding. Using acrylic paints, paint the train cars and candle cups. When dry, apply one or two coats of sealer, allowing first coat to dry before applying second. Glue the candle cups to tops of the cars.

Polar Fleece Scarf

❖ ❖ ❖ ❖ ❖

Arctic winds will not be rushing down your neck if you are wearing this cuddly warm scarf. Made from two bold shades of polar fleece with contrasting pom-poms, this scarf will keep you warm in the fiercest of gales.

Size:
Finished scarf is 48 inches (122cm) long, not including pom-poms

Materials:
¼ yard (23cm) each of two colors of polar fleece

1 50-gram (2oz) skein each of matching color sport weight yarn

Matching thread

Cardboard

Sewing machine with zizag stitch and free arm

From each color fleece, cut two 8 × 24 inch (20.5 × 61cm) pieces. Lay two same color pieces together and taper one end, beginning 6 inches (15cm) from end and narrowing to a width of 5 inches (13cm). Set machine for medium width zigzag. Overlap edges of matching color pieces by ¼ inch (6mm) along one long edge and zigzag where edges overlap. Repeat for second set of scarf pieces. Open pieces, overlap centers and seam same as before with zigzag. Starting at the middle and working out, overlap remaining long edges and zigzag along overlap. Ease the fabric along free arm as you go in order to stitch the entire length. To stitch the remaining seam you will have to leave an opening to fit around the free arm, and then stitch down to the end. Close the opening by hand.

Cut two 3-inch (7.5cm) circles from cardboard. Cut out the center of each circle leaving a ring about ⅝ to ¾-inch (1.5 to 2cm) wide. Hold rings together and wrap lengths of yarn around rings until center is completely full. Cut through edge of yarn, having bottom blade of scissors between rings if possible. Take another length of yarn and tie tightly around bundle of yarn between rings. Slip rings off, plump up yarn and trim into pom-pom shape.

By hand, gather ends of scarf, pull up tightly and sew on pom-pom of opposite color.

Polar Fleece Afghan

❖ ❖ ❖ ❖ ❖

Alternating brightly colored squares of polar fleece trimmed with black lacing and fringe makes this afghan a bold accent draped across the sofa or bed, and will keep you warm as toast when winter temperatures plummet.

Size:
45 × 55 inches (114 × 139.5cm), including fringe

Materials:
½ yard (45.5cm) each of 6 colors of polar fleece

Fine nylon monofilament thread for machine sewing

Rotary cutter

Small sharp scissors

Large-eyed tapestry needle

Transparent ruler marked in ¼-inch (6mm) increments

Sewing machine with zigzag stitch

Cut four 10-inch (25.5cm) squares from each of five colors of fleece. Mark the grain on each piece. (I pinned a piece of paper with an arrow on it to each piece.) Pieces will be sewn together in strips with the grain, then the strips sewn together across the grain.

Lay the squares out in a pleasing arrangement, four squares wide by five squares deep, being sure the grain and nap are in the same direction. With sewing machine set for wide zigzag and threaded top and bottom with nylon thread, sew squares together by butting the edges and zigzagging across the join. Assemble five strips of four squares each, then sew the strips together working from the center out, and matching seams.

With rotary cutter, cut ¼-inch (6mm) strips from sixth color of fleece, cutting with the grain. To make lacing easier, use a transparent ruler to mark the afghan for placement of holes. Holes on each side of seam should be 1 inch (2.5cm) apart and ¼ inch (6mm) from seam. After marking the first side of one seam, the holes on the opposite side of the seam should be staggered on the half-inch (1.5cm) mark. Using one blade of a small scissors, poke a hole through afghan at each mark. Thread one ¼-inch (6mm) strip through the tapestry needle and begin lacing over the seam. Use a strip about 18 inches (45.5cm) long as anything longer will deteriorate from being pulled through the holes by the time you reach the end. When one length begins to run short, use a needle and thread to join another, slightly overlapping the ends.

Working across the grain, cut four strips from sixth color of fleece, each 2½ inches (6.5cm) wide by the width of the fabric. Zigzag the ends together with nylon thread and cut ¾-inch (2cm) wide slits to make fringe. Round off corners of afghan and zigzag fringe around outside edges, securing ends of the lacing as you go.

Sources

❖ ❖ ❖ ❖ ❖

Most items used to create the projects in this book are readily available at crafts stores around the country. Here is a list of reputable mail-order suppliers with whom I have dealt.

Cherry Tree Toys, Inc.
P.O. Box 369
Belmont, OH 43718
(800) 848-4363
Stocks a wide variety of wood shapes and kits, as well as magnetic sheets and other crafts supplies.

Clotilde
2 Sew Smart Way B8031
Stevens Point, WI 55481-8031
(800) 772-2891
Stocks a wide variety of sewing supplies and accessories.

D. Blumchen & Co.
P.O. Box 1210
Ridgewood, NJ 07451-1210

Enterprise Art
P.O. Box 2918
Largo, FL 34649
(813) 536-1492
Stocks a large variety of beads as well as jewelry and some craft supplies.

The Green Pepper, Inc.
1285 River Road
Eugene, OR 97404
(503) 689-3292
Stocks a variety of outdoor fabrics, patterns, and notions.

G Street Fabrics
12240 Wilkins Avenue
Rockville, MD 20852
(301) 231-8960
Stocks a wide variety of fabrics including felt and lamé. Will supply swatches from description of your needs.

Keepsake Quilting
Route 25B
P.O. Box 1618
Centre Harbor, NH 03226-1618
(800) 525-8086
Excellent source of fabrics for crafting and sewing. Stocks several ¼-yard (23cm) collections of plaids, as well as many other patterns and accessories, including small wooden spring clothespins and tea-dyed muslin.

Nancy's Notions
333 Beichl Avenue
P.O. Box 683
Beaver Dam, WI 53916-0683
(800) 833-0690
Excellent source of sewing supplies including several fusible webs, fusible fleece, battings, polar fleece, clear vinyl, and metallic threads.

Newark Dressmaker Supply
6473 Ruch Road
P.O. Box 20730
Lehigh Valley, PA 18002-0730
(610) 837-7500
Stocks a variety of craft and sewing supplies, including 14-count plastic canvas.

Patternworks
P.O. Box 1690
Poughkeepsie, NY 12601
(914) 462-8000
Stocks a wide variety of yarns as well as knit and crochet accessories.

The Rain Shed
707 NW 11th
Corvallis, OR 97330
(503) 753-8900
Stocks a variety of outdoor fabrics, such as polar fleece, and notions that work with them.

Thorburn's
123 Nashua Road
Suite 128
Londonderry, NH 03053-3465
(603) 437-4924
Stocks an excellent selection of polar fleece and other outdoor fabrics.

Index

❖ ❖ ❖ ❖ ❖